Florida

By Carmen Bredeson

Consultant
Nanci Vargus, Ed.D.
Primary Multiage Teacher
Decatur Township Schools, Indianapolis, Indiana

Children's Press®
A Division of Scholastic Inc.
New York   Toronto   London   Auckland   Sydney
Mexico City   New Delhi   Hong Kong
Danbury, Connecticut

Designer: Herman Adler Design
Photo Researcher: Caroline Anderson
The photo on the cover shows a beach in Florida.

Library of Congress Cataloging-in-Publication Data

Bredeson, Carmen.
  Florida / by Carmen Bredeson.
    p. cm. — (Rookie read-about geography)
  Includes index.
  Summary: Introduces the state of Florida and its diverse geographical
features, interesting sights, agricultural crops, wildlife, and cities.
  ISBN 0-516-22671-1 (lib. bdg.)   0-516-27498-8 (pbk.)
  1. Florida—Juvenile literature. 2. Florida—Geography—Juvenile literature.
[1. Florida.] I. Title. II. Series.
  F311.3 .B74 2002
  917.59—dc21
                                        2002005492

Do you know why Florida is called the Sunshine State?

4

The weather there is warm and sunny.

Florida is located in the southeast part of the United States. Can you find Florida on this map?

Florida is a peninsula. It is connected to the United States on only one side. The rest of the state has water all around it. The Atlantic Ocean is on the east side. The Gulf of Mexico is on the west side.

ALABAMA

GEORGIA

ATLANTIC
OCEAN

FLORIDA

GULF OF
MEXICO

North
West — East
South

Florida Keys

There are sandy beaches in Florida. Seashells wash onto the shore with the waves. Dolphins swim by in the warm water.

Florida has many forests.

Gray foxes, birds, deer,
and wildcats live here. The
mockingbird is Florida's
state bird. It builds nests
in the tall trees.

The largest swamp in
Florida is in Everglades
National Park. A swamp
is an area of land that is
wet and spongy.

Many alligators and snakes
live in this huge swamp.

Mangrove trees grow in the swampy areas of Florida. These trees have roots that grow above the ground.

Spoonbills build their nests
in these trees.

There are thousands of lakes in Florida. The largest is Lake Okeechobee. This big lake is found in the southern part of Florida.

The Florida Keys are found off the southern coast of Florida. Many people visit these warm islands. The coral reef along the Florida Keys is an underwater state park.

19

People who live in Florida work in national parks, hotels, and theme parks like Walt Disney World.

Many people live in cities along the coast. Miami is a big city at the southern tip of Florida.

Ranchers and farmers live
in the Florida countryside.
Ranchers raise cattle
and hogs.

Farmers grow sugarcane,
oranges, and other crops.

Tallahassee is the capital of Florida. This is where the state government makes laws. You can visit the Governor's Mansion in Tallahassee.

27

What is your favorite place in Florida?

Words You Know

beach

coral reef

Florida

Lake Okeechobee

mangrove trees

Miami

sugarcane

swamp

31

Index

About the Author

Carmen Bredeson is the author of twenty-five books for children. She lives in Texas and enjoys doing research and traveling.

Photo Credits

Photographs © 2002: Corbis Images/Kevin Fleming: 16, 30 bottom right; H. Armstrong Roberts, Inc.: 3, 23, 31 top right (R. Benson), 12, 31 bottom right (W. Bertsch), 27 (M. Landre), 10, 25, 31 bottom left (W. Metzen); Photo Researchers, NY: 13 (David N. Davis), 8, 30 top left (Jeff Greenberg), 14, 31 top left (L. Newman & A. Flowers); Superstock, Inc.: 20; The Image Bank/Getty Images: cover; Visuals Unlimited: 28 (Jeff Greenberg), 11 (R. Lindholm), 15 (A. Morris), 19, 30 top right (Rick Poley), 24 (William J. Weber).

Maps by Bob Italiano